D0127549

Encore!

Encore!

For Teresa!

Published by:
Rubes Publications
14447 Titus St.
Panorama City, CA 91402

ENCORE!

Library of Congress Catalog Card Number:
83-090153

ISBN: 0-943384-03-6

Book Design by Great American Print Machine I
Photography by Teresa LeDesma
Calligraphy by Reuben Allen
Printed in the United States of America

FIRST PRINTING OCTOBER 1983
SECOND PRINTING JANUARY 1984
THIRD PRINTING JUNE 1984

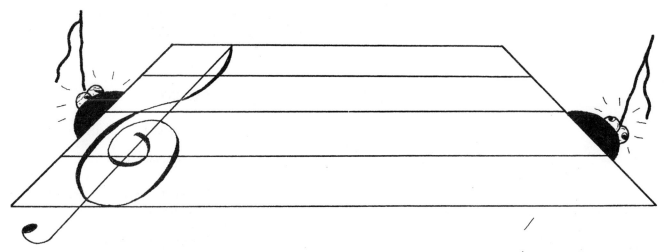

"I knew we shouldn't try to carry a tune by ourselves."

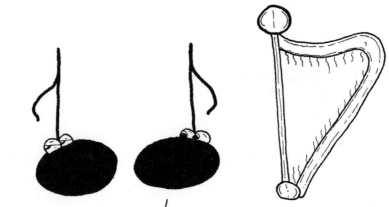

"Wow! I've never played to a full house."

"So I see you've taken up the accordian."

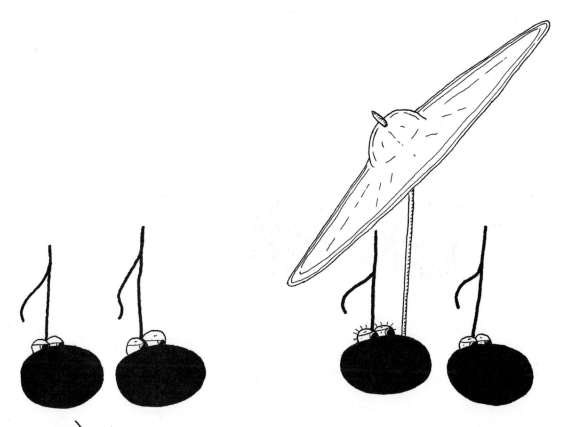

"I know they really can't afford it. Besides, it's a silly status cymbal."

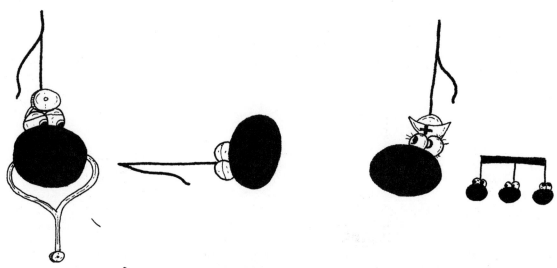

"Maybe he wasn't expecting triplets."

"Stop fretting and relax. You're too high strung."

"Sure being a D.J. has its ups and downs but it's worth being on the air."

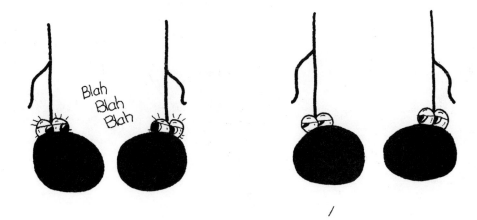

"Between my wife and my mother-in-law I get nagged in stereo."

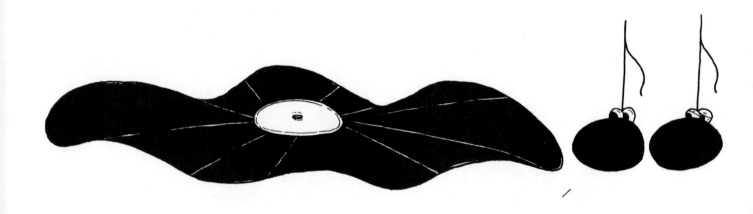

"Once it's warped..., it's hard to set the record straight."

"Well Maw, looks like a great harvest. We better get a pluckin."

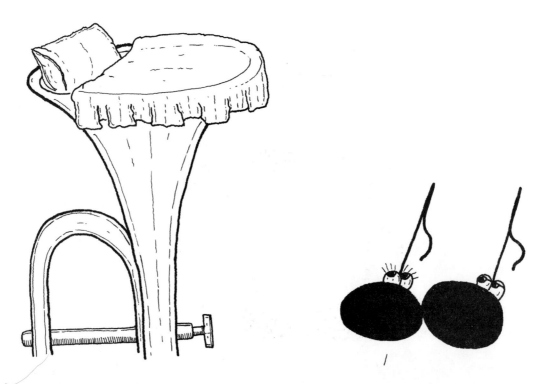

"Oh darling, a brass bed! It's just what I've always wanted!"

"I told you to use the restroom before we left home!"

"Bellboy, show this guest to the Nutcracker Suite."

"Some watchdog! All he does is sit around and listen to music!"

"When I said take it from the top, I meant the song!"

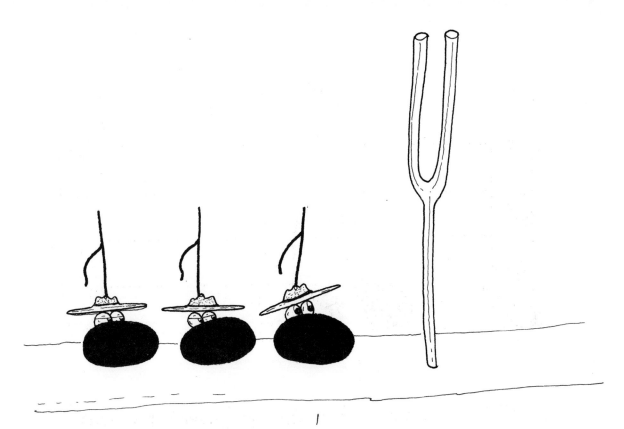

"Now what do we do? The map didn't say anything about a fork in the road!"

"Listen kid, before you score a hit, you have to learn how to swing."

"If you don't want a solo arrangement, stop taking all the sheets."

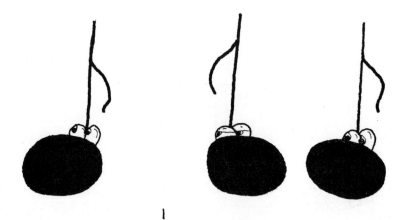

"Sure, Brahms is a nice guy, but personally his music puts me to sleep."

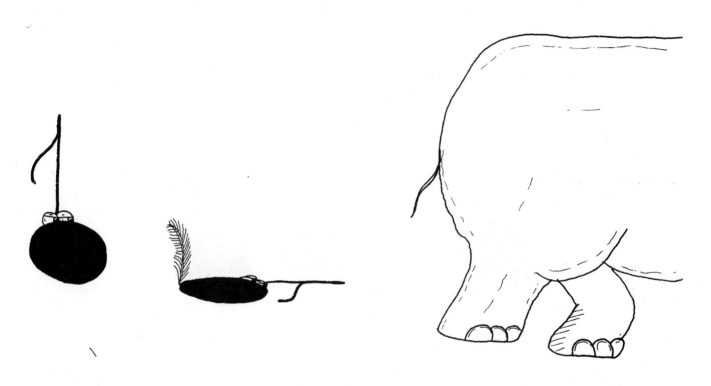

"Next time you tickle the ivories, make sure they're on a piano."

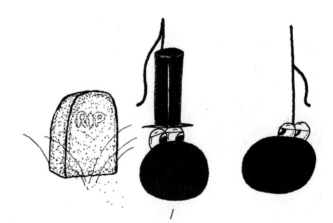

"To be frank, I'm tired of working with dead beats."

"Four score and seven years ago..."

"Yes, I'm sick of the same old grind too."

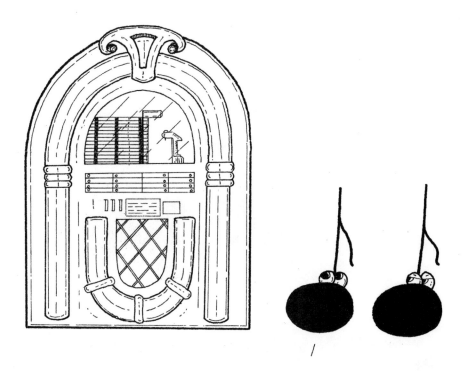

"Hey! I hear this is where the singles play."

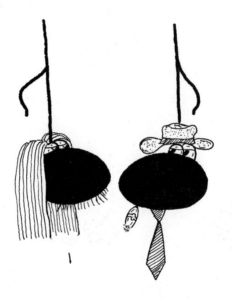

"Face it, Pop,... you and I walk to the beat of a different drum."

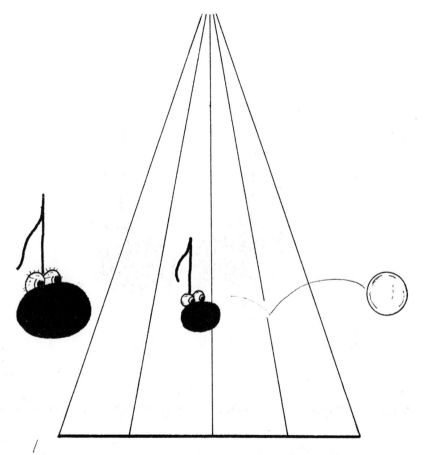

"I told you not to follow the bouncing ball into the street!"

"Before you take the stand, do you swear to tell the whole truth?"

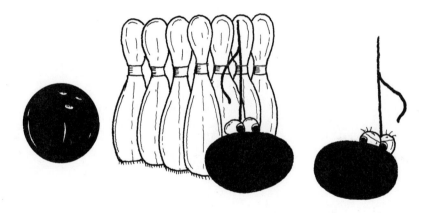

"I thought you were taking me to the <u>Hollywood Bowl</u>!"

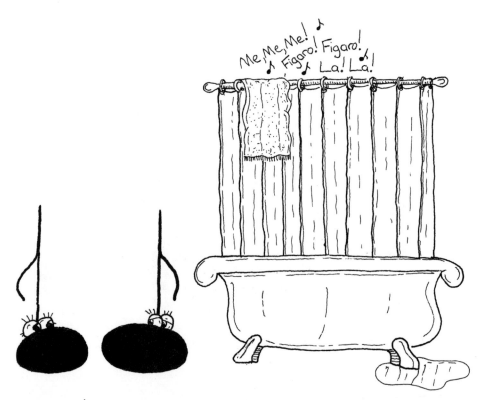

"He calls it 'singing in the shower,... I call it *soapy opera*."

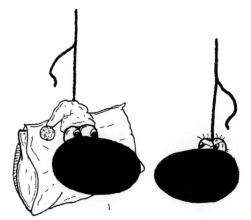

"Well, you told me to get ready for a <u>night</u> at the opera!"

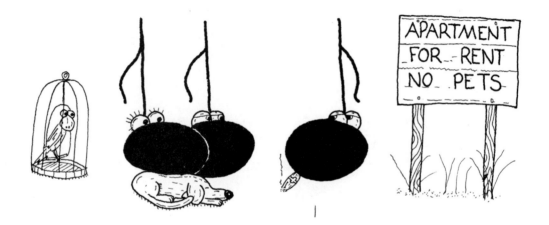

"You saw the sign,"<u>No Pets!</u>", that includes woofers and tweeters!"

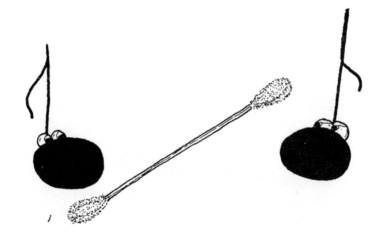

"Here's a little tip for when you play by ear."

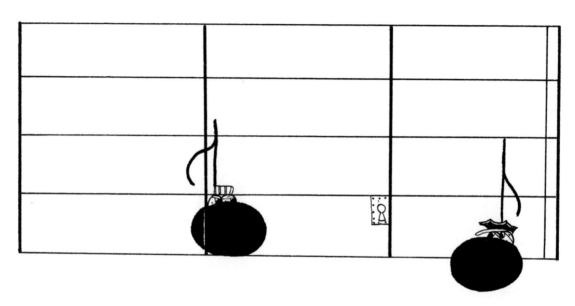

"Sure it's bad behind bars,...but did they have to send me to Sing Sing?"

" To Be Bop or not to Be Bop,... <u>that</u> is the question!"

"Looks like the great conductor got some thunderous applause."

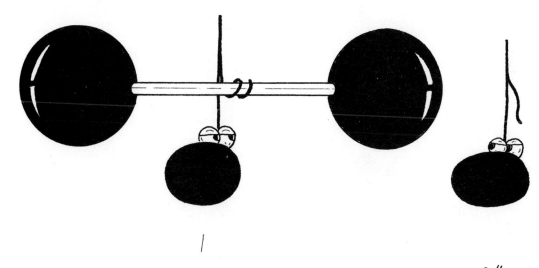

"If you think heavy metal is so easy, why don't you try it?"

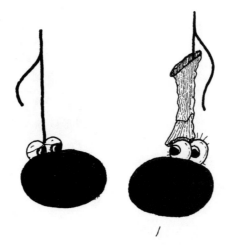

"Without jazzercise I don't know how I'd keep in tone."

"Now son, if you don't stop skipping, you'll ruin your record!"

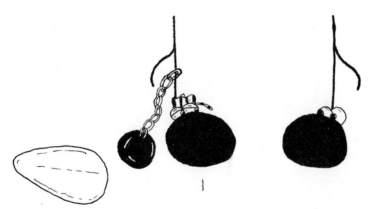

"The judge threw me a pick and gave me twenty years at hard rock."

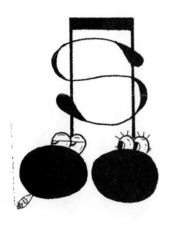

"It's obvious why she married him."

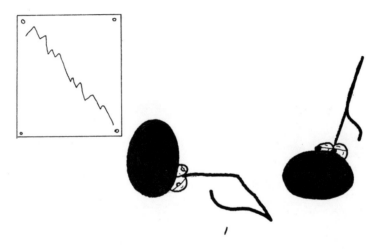

"According to the record charts, it appears you have a slipped disc."

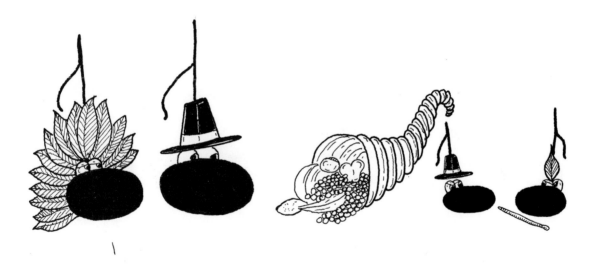

"I dont understand why they fight over a drumstick, we have plenty of food."

"I once loved a flutist, but we split because the trill was gone!"

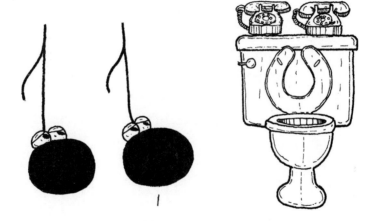

" I've heard of headphones, but this is ridiculous."

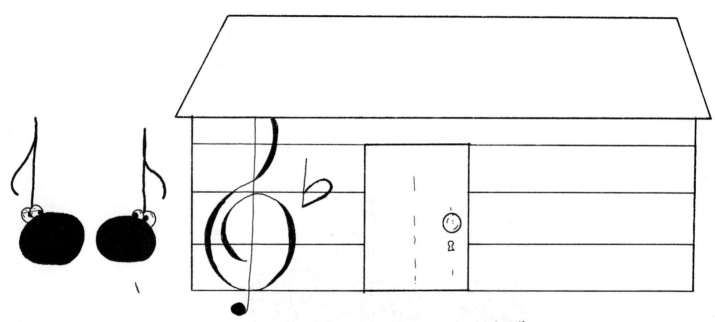

"My wife locked me out and changed the key!"

"Sure, I can turn any record into gold... all I need is $500,000.00 for promotion!"

"Your fear of chamber music stems from an acute case of claustrophobia."

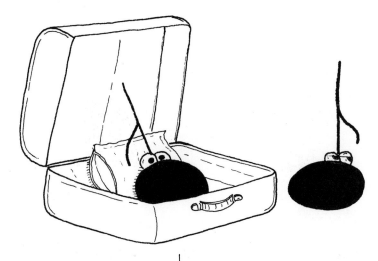

"I don't mind being on tour, but living out of a suitcase wears me out."

"Life is like a player piano, you have to roll with the punches."

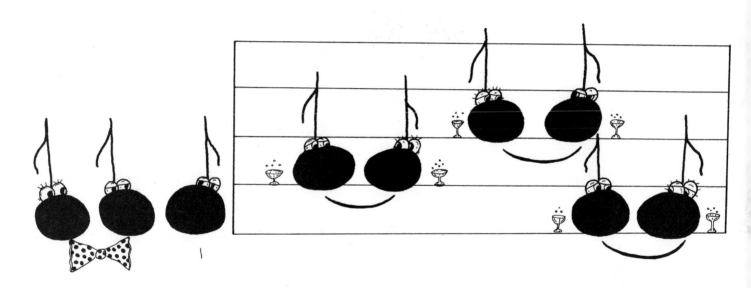

"I'm sorry sir, this restaurant is strictly black tie."

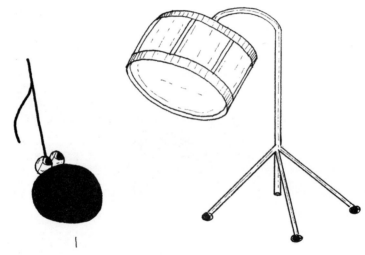

"Well, if you didn't feel beat, you wouldn't be doing your job."

"If this is light opera, why does my co-star weigh 300 pounds?"

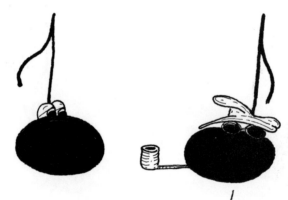

"Old musicians never die, they just decompose."

"It's painfully obvious that he's gone commercial."

No, no, no,!!! I said I <u>want</u> <u>to</u> boogie man!

"It's lovely, but it's not what I had in mind for a choral arrangement."

"Personally, I'm sick of Beatlemania."

∴..But Doc, nature just didn't intend for us to be synthesized!"

"There must be an easier way to get in tune besides yoga!"

"It's a stereotype to think all notes have rhythm."

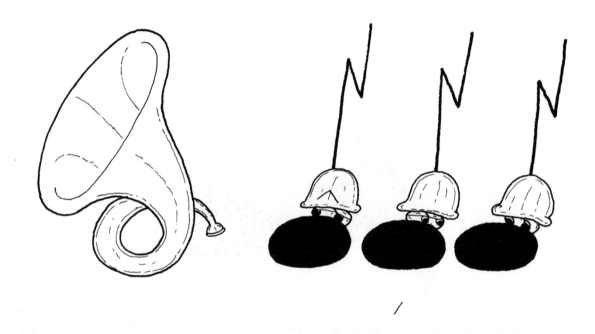

"Personally, I think the top brass is full of hot air."

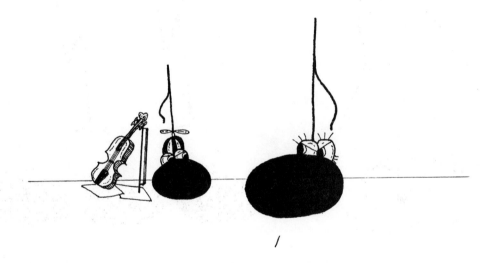

"You'll never be a great violinist if you keep fiddling around."

"Why should I sell out? I'm happy being Baroque."

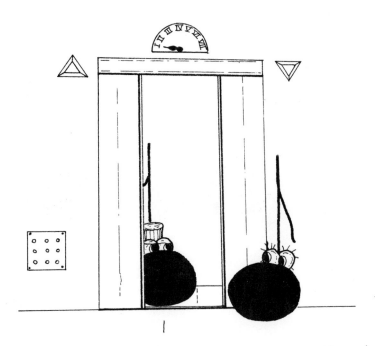

"I don't mind playing elevator music, but I got the shaft."

"Sure he plays great jazz, but he doesn't have to keep blowing his own horn."

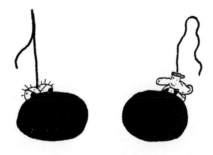

"It's no wonder you're hungover. Last nite you got so high you shattered all the glasses!"

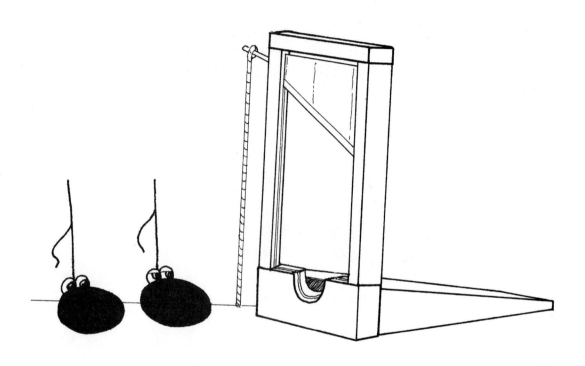

"This should keep the music critics quiet."

"No,...it's not hard to unwind after working in a music box all day."

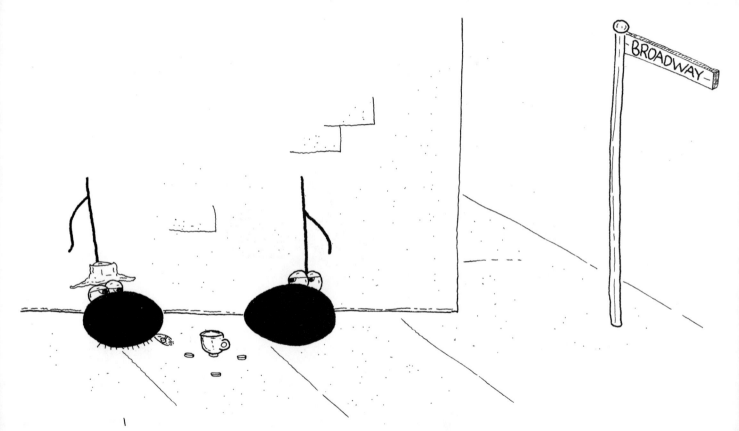

"How would you like to support the arts and donate to an off Broadway musician?"

"When you said he was <u>radioactive</u>, I thought he got a lot of <u>airplay</u>!"

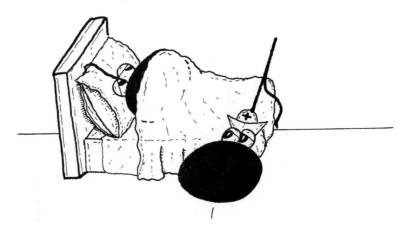

"Removing an organ doesn't mean you'll never play the piano again."

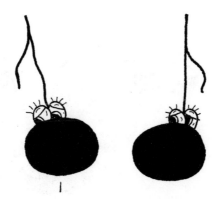

"I'll never let a musician play me again!"

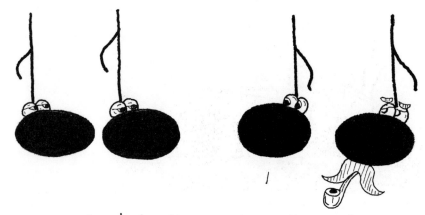

"You guys go ahead to the movies. I'll spend an evening at the Pop's."

"You might say that last encore <u>really</u> brought the house down."

THE ORIGINAL BEST SELLER!

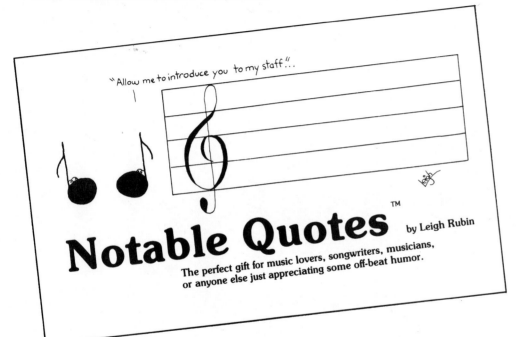

"Allow me to introduce you to my staff."...

Notable Quotes ™
by Leigh Rubin

The perfect gift for music lovers, songwriters, musicians, or anyone else just appreciating some off-beat humor.

If you thought those little critters called musical notes were only good for coming up with melody and tone just wait until they beat against your funny bone.